*The Da Vinci Code*
*from*
*Dan Brown's Fiction*
*to*
*Mary Magdalene's Faith*

# The Da Vinci Code

## From Dan Brown's Fiction
### to
### Mary Magdalene's Faith

## GARRY WILLIAMS

**CHRISTIAN FOCUS**

ISBN 1-84550-121-7

10 9 8 7 6 5 4

Copyright © Garry Williams 2006

Published in 2006
by
Christian Focus Publications,
Geanies House, Fearn, Ross-shire,
IV20 1TW, Scotland

www.christianfocus.com

Cover design by Alister MacInnes
(www.moose77.com)

Printed and bound by
Norhaven A/S Paperback, Denmark

# Contents

# To the Reader

*I* have written this short book for anyone who has been intrigued by Dan Brown's portrayal of Jesus Christ, Mary Magdalene, and the church in his book *The Da Vinci Code*.

If you are a real *Da Vinci Code* hack then there are plenty of books to keep you busy that are longer and more detailed than this. With the help of a range of authors from quite different perspectives you can get behind it, you can unlock it, you can crack it, you can break it, you can de-code it. For many readers, however, the interest is real, but it is not sufficient to sustain such detailed reading. As I surveyed the range of books available, it occurred to me that a shorter treatment might actually be more accessible for many readers, even if only as a starting point. So if you would appreciate a piece which interacts with Dan Brown's story in a more succinct fashion, then I hope that you will enjoy what I have written here.

This book is also for you if you have been made to think about the identities of Jesus Christ and Mary Magdalene afresh by reading the novel.

For many today, the New Testament is a dim memory from childhood and school, if that. You may recall rewriting the parables in a modern setting, but not much more. You might ask yourself, for example, when you last sat down as an adult and read through one of the Gospels from beginning to end. It can be done in little more than an hour, but increasingly many adults have not done it for years, if ever. Yet perhaps *The Da Vinci Code* has rekindled an interest in this man Jesus

Christ. Perhaps you have been made to think again, to ask who he was, to ponder on what he said and did. Jesus himself once asked his disciples: 'Who do you say that I am?'. For many people Dan Brown has put that supremely important question back on the agenda. If it is a question on which you have found yourself musing, then considering the argument of this piece may prove to be for you more than just an enjoyable read.

If you would like to look up my references to the text as you read, they are from the 2004 edition of *The Da Vinci Code* by Dan Brown, published by Bantam Press/Corgi. The material is reprinted by permission of The Random House Group Ltd.

# Chapter 1

## Mary Magdalene: Wife?

THE PHENOMENON OF *THE DA VINCI CODE*

*T*here can be no mistaking the fact that Dan Brown's *The Da Vinci Code* is a hugely successful novel. The facts speak for themselves. A short while ago it was being translated into more than forty languages. As I write it is being made into a film starring Tom Hanks. At the end of 2004 it had reportedly earned Brown £140,000,000, an amount so large that it is hard to imagine how one might spend it. On 17th July 2005 the British newspaper *The Independent* recorded that 25,000,000 copies of the book had been sold in forty-four languages. Most of the early reviews of the book were gushingly positive. *The New York Times*, quoted inside the front of the book, tells us that the word for *The Da Vinci Code* is 'wow'. In what was presumably meant to be a compliment, *Salon. com* describes it as 'the pulp must-read of the season'.

It is obvious why people like the book. Dan Brown, a teacher of creative writing, has done his homework, and he has mastered the formula for writing page-turners. There are many things which have been said in criticism of the literary standards of the novel, but *The Da Vinci Code* is a very good example of the kind of book that people enjoy on holiday, lying on the beach, being entertained and happily turning the pages. There is also more to it than this, since it contains intriguing ideas about history and religion. Indeed, some readers may feel as if they have been initiated into a great global secret that stretches back for centuries, a secret that discloses something extraordinary about Jesus Christ and the history of the church, especially the Roman Catholic Church.

Others, however, have a completely different opinion of *The Da Vinci Code*, and have expressed some extremely negative verdicts on it. A review in *The Sunday Telegraph* declared that 'Brown's book is not garbage, it is garbage on stilts, hyper-garbage that invokes garbage in self-authentication' (21st November, 2004). In their own book about the book, *The Da Vinci Hoax*, Carl Olson and Sandra Miesel write that *The Da Vinci Code* 'is custom-made fiction for our time: pretentious, posturing, self-serving, arrogant, self-congratulatory, condescending, glib, illogical, superficial, and deviant' (p. 296).

So why is it that many people do not like the book? Literary merits aside, the key reason for the negative reaction to the book is that people object to the way in which it presents an alternative history of Jesus Christ and the church. It is this rewriting of history that will be our focus here.

COME ON, DON'T TAKE IT SO SERIOUSLY!

At the outset though, I need to face a thought that may spring up in your mind. Surely, you might say, it is just a story, a novel, fiction. Why spend time treating it as if it were a history book? Let me give you four reasons why I don't think we can take such a dismissive approach.

First of all, that is not how lots of readers are taking it. People, like it or not – believe it or not! – are concluding that the book tells us the truth about what Jesus Christ really did and taught, or at least throws up sufficient dust to discredit the Bible's accounts. On the BBC website, for example, Steven from Sheffield asked: 'If so many people believe it to be true, then how can it be fiction?'. And he is not alone. These kinds of comments are not exactly profound, but they do show how many readers are viewing the novel.

Secondly, and perhaps with less excuse, many reviewers are taking the novel in the same way. It is hailed in a number of the reviews quoted inside the front cover as an 'intelligent' novel. The *Chicago Tribune* describes the book as 'brain candy of the highest quality' which, it assures us, is a great story 'despite transmitting several doctorates' worth of fascinating history and learned speculation'.

Third, Dan Brown himself takes the key claims of his work as history, not as fiction. On Jesus and Mary Magdalene being married, *The Washington Post* quotes him as saying this: 'I was sceptical, but after a year and a half of research I became a believer' (20th July, 2003). And on *Good Morning America* he said something similar: 'I really thought I would disprove a lot of this theory about Mary Magdalene and Holy Blood and all of that. I became a believer' (*Breaking the Da Vinci Code*, p. 3). Perhaps he is saying this just to push up sales, but this is still how people are being encouraged to take the book.

Lastly, there are the books behind the book. Brown's picture of history is very largely based on a number of other books published over the last twenty or so years, especially a book by Michael Baigent, Richard Leigh, and Henry Lincoln entitled *The Holy Blood and the Holy Grail*. This book, which Brown cites as a source, is not a novel: it claims to be an exposé, revealing startling discoveries about the true history of Jesus Christ and the church.

For these four reasons it is appropriate to take *The Da Vinci Code* as a work purporting to make true historical claims, and to scrutinize it as such.

## DOES DAN BROWN REALLY KNOW HIS HISTORY?

I do not like 'machine gun' arguments, the kind where someone fires out so many bullets that it is hard to keep track of them, let alone to reply to them properly. Even so, we'll begin that way! Just as an initial warning sign, we need to note that there are numerous simple and yet serious errors of fact throughout the book. These simple errors indicate that Brown is in fact piecing together bits from other books without knowing the material properly himself. Certainly that is what the authors who have apparently sued him for intellectual theft seem to be implying. Let me rattle through some examples.

Brown says that the Dead Sea Scrolls together with the Nag Hammadi texts are 'the earliest Christian records' (p. 331). But the scrolls never mention Jesus or anything Christian. Brown says that the divinity of Jesus was established at the Council of Nicaea by 'a relatively close vote' (p. 315). But only two out of the 250 or so bishops voted against the creed. Brown says that

Pope Clement V threw the remains of burnt Templars into the River Tiber which is in Rome (p. 447). But Clement was Pope from 1305-14 and fixed his residence at Avignon; he never went to Rome. Brown says that the 'nuns' of the Confraternity of the Immaculate Conception gave instructions for the *Madonna of the Rocks* painting (p. 191). But there were no nuns in the order – it was an all male group.

Lastly, Brown says that the documents in the Paris Bibliothèque Nationale which tell of the Priory of Sion, the *Dossier Secrets*, 'had been authenticated by many specialists' (p. 280). But they are a hoax. This was exposed some years ago by French journalist Jean-Luc Chaumeil. He published books on the subject, and even the BBC put out a documentary outlining the hoax in 1996. The forger of the texts himself, Philippe de Chérisey, admitted in a collection of papers that they were fakes. Given the importance of the Priory in Brown's reconstruction of events, given its key role as custodian of the bloodline of Jesus, this is a terminal blow to Brown's alternative history. The entire later phase of Brown's history, from the supposed foundation of the Priory in

1099, is knocked out when these documents are exposed as fakes.

Here then are some basic mistakes which Brown makes. There are many more, as any number of books on the subject will show. Having exposed a hole in the story from 1099 to the present, we will now rewind further back to consider seven of Brown's key claims about the early church and Jesus.

## CLAIM 1

Claim 1 is that the New Testament canon, the list of books to be counted as Christian Scripture alongside the Old Testament, was created by Constantine who rejected thousands of alternative texts by the Gnostics. Brown writes: 'The fundamental irony of Christianity! The Bible, as we know it today, was collated by the pagan Roman emperor Constantine the Great' (p. 313).

This is not true. Constantine did ask bishop Eusebius of Caesarea to have fifty copies of the New Testament reproduced for the new imperial capital at Constantinople. But the work of collating the New Testament books had been done over the preceding centuries. The evidence for this is abundant.

The most famous documentary example is a piece of writing known as the Muratorian fragment. This fragment dates from the end of the second century and is named after the Italian scholar who first published it in 1740. It is a list of books recognized by the church: four Gospels (though the first two are missing due to damage to the fragment), the Acts of the Apostles, thirteen epistles of Paul; three epistles of John; Jude; the Apocalypses of John and Peter. Significantly, the Muratorian canon rejects Gnostic works by Valentinus and others. This is important for showing that Brown is wrong, because it proves that as early as the end of the second century the church was already denying the truth of Gnosticism, and the canon of Scripture was being formed.

## CLAIM 2

Claim 2 is that the four Gospels were selected by Constantine from eighty others. Brown writes: 'Constantine commissioned and financed a new Bible, which omitted those gospels that spoke of Christ's *human* traits and embellished those gospels that made Him godlike. The earlier gospels were outlawed, gathered up, and burned' (p. 317). Or again: 'More than *eighty* gospels were considered for the New Testament, and yet only a relative few were chosen for inclusion' (p. 313).

This is wrong. Many early Christian texts written well before Constantine's time say that there are and can be only four authoritative Gospels. Irenaeus, who died in around AD200, over a century before Constantine's reign, writes this in his great work *Against the Heresies*:

> It is not possible that the Gospels can be either more or fewer in number than they are. For, since there are four zones of the world in which we live, and four principal winds, while the church is scattered throughout all the world [...] it is fitting that she should have four pillars [...]. From which fact, it is evident that the Word, [...] who was manifested to men, has given us the Gospel under four aspects, but bound together by one Spirit. (III. xi. 8; *Ante-Nicene Fathers*, 1:428)

This may seem like a strange argument to us – four winds so four Gospels – but the point is clear. There is no evidence that there were ever anywhere near eighty Gospels, and the selection was made many years before Constantine was even born.

## CLAIM 3

Claim 3 is that at the Council of Nicaea the Emperor Constantine rejected the earthly Jesus and made him divine for the first time. Brown writes on Nicaea: 'until *that* moment in history, Jesus was viewed by His followers as a mortal prophet…a great and powerful man, but a *man* nonetheless. A mortal.' Or again on the same page: 'Constantine turned Jesus into a deity who existed beyond the scope of the human world, an entity whose power was unchallengeable' (p. 315).

Some of this is true. Certainly the Council of Nicaea did assert that Jesus was fully God. But Brown is wrong in two ways here. First of all, belief in the full divinity of Jesus was present from the outset of the Christian faith, not just from the time of Constantine and Nicaea. The letters of Paul, for example, written in the first century, show that the early Christians believed that Jesus was God. Paul speaks of Jesus in a way that a

Jew would only speak of God. He calls him 'Lord (*kurios*)', the word used of God in the Old Testament, and he applies Old Testament texts to Jesus that speak about God himself. A good example occurs in his description of Jesus in Philippians 2:9-11:

> Therefore God exalted him to the highest place and gave him the name that is above every name, that at the name of Jesus every knee should bow, in heaven and on earth and under the earth, and every tongue confess that Jesus Christ is Lord, to the glory of God the Father.

Here Paul applies to Jesus Christ words that in the prophecy of Isaiah in the Old Testament refer to God alone:

> Turn to me and be saved, all you ends of the earth; for I am God, and there is no other. By myself have I sworn, my mouth has uttered in all integrity a word that will not be revoked: Before me every knee will bow; by me every tongue will swear. (Isaiah 45:22-23)

Lest we think that this was just something that Paul invented, we may note the many ways in which the Gospels themselves indicate the divinity of Jesus. In Mark 1:1-3, for example, we find a similar application to Jesus of an Old Testament text about God. John the Baptist comes to prepare the way for Jesus, but we read that in the desert he proclaimed 'Prepare the way for the Lord, make straight paths for him'. This is a quotation from Isaiah 40:3, where the 'Lord' is God himself. John prepared for Jesus, which in itself *was* preparing for God.

Christian literature from just after New Testament times also speaks of Jesus plainly as God. Ignatius of Antioch (who had died by about 107), wrote this of Jesus to the church at Ephesus:

'Very Flesh, yet Spirit too;
Uncreated, and yet born;
God-and-Man in One agreed'
(§7; *Early Christian Writings*, p. 63)

Secondly, Brown is wrong when he claims that the four Gospels downplay the humanity and mortality of Jesus. This is an incredible claim, since it makes absolutely no sense of what we find in the Gospels. John declares emphatically that 'the Word became flesh' (1:14). Jesus in the Gospels is born, grows, eats, sleeps, is in agony, weeps, and dies. The Gospels actually seek to show that Jesus was a man.

There is a great irony here. Brown accuses the Gospels of denying the true humanity of Jesus, but it was the Gnostics, the authors of those other gospels that Brown favours, who denied the humanity of Jesus. This is Gnosticism 101: anyone who knows anything about Gnosticism knows this. Far from the Gnostics being wonderfully in favour of earthly existence, they were the ones who hated the flesh. They propagated a heresy which denied the true humanity of Jesus and held that he only appeared to be human (hence it was known as 'docetism', from the Greek verb *dokeō*, 'to seem'). It was not Constantine who came up with this heresy, it was the Gnostics. In one passage in the *Apocalypse of Peter*, for example, the Gnostics describe the body of Jesus on the cross suffering, but then describe the real Jesus, watching and laughing at what was happening:

> The Savior said to me, 'He whom you saw on the tree, glad and laughing, this is the living Jesus. But this one into whose hands

and feet they drive the nails is his fleshly
part, which is the substitute being put to
shame, the one who came into being in his
likeness. But look at him and me. (§81; *The
Nag Hammadi Library*, p. 377).

CLAIM 4

We come to another irony with Claim 4,
that the Gnostics were the guardians of the
heritage of the sacred feminine. For many
of his women readers this may be one of the
most appealing aspects of Brown's book.
Yet again this is an amazing picture of
Gnosticism. In fact, though Gnosticism did
describe feminine elements in the divine
realm, it was overwhelmingly hostile to
women. For example, where the Apostle Paul
singles out the first man, Adam, for blame
when he speaks of the fall of the world into
sin (Romans 5:12-21), many of the Gnostics
blame the feminine spiritual being Sophia.
She was the one who could not control her
desire and who disrupted the cosmos, as a
result producing what the Gnostics think of
as our evil material world. But the portrayal
of the feminine in Gnosticism gets worse than
this. Let me quote how the Jesus depicted in

the Gnostic Gospel of Thomas speaks of Mary Magdalene at the climax of the Gospel:

> Simon Peter said to them, 'Let Mary leave us, for women are not worthy of life.' Jesus said, 'I myself shall lead her in order to make her male, so that she too may become a living spirit resembling you males. For every woman who will make herself male will enter the kingdom of heaven.' (Saying 114; *The Nag Hammadi Library*, p. 138)

Feminists indeed! The mention of women brings us to the next claim and closer to the woman at the centre of *The Da Vinci Code*.

CLAIM 5

Claim 5 is that Jesus had to be married. Brown writes: 'the social decorum during that time virtually forbade a Jewish man to be unmarried. According to Jewish custom, celibacy was condemned, and the obligation for a Jewish father was to find a suitable wife for his son' (p. 330).

While marriage was clearly the norm for Jewish men in the time of Jesus, it was not the case that a Jewish man had to be married. Indeed, there were notable precedents for respectable singleness among Jewish men. Many of the Essenes, the group connected with the Dead Sea Scrolls, were noted for their celibacy, and were at the same time respected for their holiness (Josephus, *War* 2.8.2.121-122; *Antiquities* 18.1.5.20-21). If this was the case with the Essenes, then it certainly could have been the case with Jesus.

## CLAIM 6

Claim 6 is the more specific assertion that Jesus was married to a particular woman, Mary Magdalene. Brown writes: 'the marriage of Jesus and Mary Magdalene is part of the historical record' (p. 330). Despite this assertion, Brown only cites one piece of significant ancient evidence, a passage from the Gospel of Philip, one of the Gnostic gospels not included in the New Testament. Here is how he quotes the text:

> And the companion of the Saviour is Mary Magdalene. Christ loved her more than all the disciples and used to kiss her often on her mouth. The rest of the disciples were offended by it and expressed disapproval. They said to him, 'Why do you love her more than all of us?' (p. 331)

Teabing comments: 'As any Aramaic scholar will tell you, the word companion, in those days, literally meant spouse' (p. 331).

So here is the sum of the evidence: one text, and the fact that the word 'companion' means 'spouse'. That is it. He cites no other evidence which actually makes this bold claim. This is because there is no other evidence. So how good is the evidence he does cite?

First, we need to note that while the New Testament Gospels were written during the first century AD, the Gospel of Philip was most likely written in the second half of the third century, that is, after 250. This is significant. Which has more credibility, the New Testament Gospels, written well before the end of the first century within decades of the life of Jesus, or a text written over 220 years after he lived?

Secondly, we need to quote what the text of the Gospel of Philip actually says. Note how the following quotation, which is taken from the scholarly edition of the Gospel, is actually much more uncertain and fragmentary than Brown's quotation suggests. Each set of brackets in the text marks a gap in the manuscript, and each word within the brackets is the editor's attempt at reconstructing what should be there:

> And the companion of the [...] Mary Magdalene. [...loved] her more than [all] the disciples [and used to] kiss her [often] on her [...]. The rest of [the disciples...]. They said to him, 'Why do you love her more than all of us?' (§§63-4; *The Nag Hammadi Library*, p. 148)

Thirdly, Brown is simply wrong about the meaning of 'companion'. The text of the Gospel of Philip which we have is in Coptic, but the word used here, *koinōnos*, is borrowed from the Greek language. In Greek, the word can mean 'spouse', but it is not the normal word that would have been used for a wife. It can also mean a host of other things. In Luke 5:10 it is used to describe the relation between fishermen who worked together as business partners. In Matthew 23:30 Jesus uses it to describe how the Pharisees deny that they would have been fellow-murderers with those who killed the prophets. There are, in other words, plenty of non-sexual meanings for the word. To say that Mary was

Jesus's 'companion' need say nothing at all about a sexual relationship.

But what about the kiss? Does the kiss not prove that it must be the sexual sense of the word intended here? Hardly. A little earlier in the Gospel of Philip (§59) we read of how the Gnostics would kiss one another, clearly indicating that this was a regular practice. In short, there is no ancient evidence that Jesus was married to Mary.

There is of course other more recent evidence used in *The Da Vinci Code* to suggest that Mary was married to Jesus and even bore his child, most notably Leonardo Da Vinci's painting *The Last Supper*. It may be worth commenting on this supposed evidence here. Brown claims that two key aspects in the painting signal the relationship between Mary and Jesus. First, he points to the appearance of the person sitting on Jesus's right (his left as you look at the picture). The person has long red hair and, it is claimed, the figure of a woman. Brown argues that this is not the Apostle John, which is the traditional identification, but Mary (pp. 318-30). Secondly, a major clue for Brown is the absence of any single cup or grail on the table. He claims that this points to the true grail being not a single cup, but the woman herself. Where the cup would have contained wine representing the blood of Jesus, here the woman is in place of the cup. She is the container or vessel for the blood of Jesus. Hence she forms a V shape with Jesus, a symbol of the chalice (p. 329). How could this be? Only if she contains in her womb the bloodline, the child, of Jesus (pp. 335-6).

There are other points which Brown makes to support this reading of the painting, but these are the central elements. None of them withstands scrutiny. For the absence of a single cup to have the considerable significance which Brown gives it, it would need to be an unusual feature of paintings from the time. Yet among Italian paintings of the Last Supper from the years 1300-1500, around one third have no single chalice. This means that we see in Leonardo's painting simply a standard option for depicting the final meal that Jesus ate with his disciples, not a sign pointing us to a secret.

Just as awareness of the art of the time undermines Brown's use of the absent grail, so too awareness of Leonardo's own paintings undermines his identification of the person beside Jesus as Mary. Leonardo often painted men who looked remarkably like women, so that the feminine depiction of John here cannot be taken to indicate more than Leonardo's penchant for feminine-looking men in his paintings. You can see the evidence for this simply by looking at his painting *St John the Baptist*, which depicts the normally rough-edged Baptist in a distinctly womanly form. It is available online, for example at www.wga.hu. As for the V shape, if you look closely enough you will find that you can discover a surprising number of letters in the picture, if you go looking for them.

CLAIM 7

Claim 7 is that Mary was demonized to discredit her claim to be the companion of Jesus. Brown writes: 'The Church, in order to defend itself against the Magdalene's power, perpetuated her image as a whore and buried evidence of Christ's marriage to her' (p. 340).

This claim does not fit the evidence of history. When the church did come to view

Mary as a prostitute, it did not do so as the result of some great conspiracy. Rather, it did so simply because the text of Luke's Gospel can be read that way very easily. At the end of Luke 7 we read of a prostitute being forgiven, then at the start of Luke 8 we are introduced to Mary Magdalene. Luke does *not* say that the prostitute was Mary. So the New Testament, meant to be part of the conspiracy against Mary, never makes the move of identifying her as a prostitute. Yet it was an easy move to make on literary grounds, albeit mistaken. In fact the identification seems first to have been made by Pope Gregory in the year 591, which does not fit Brown's picture of an ancient conspiracy to marginalize Mary.

Much more importantly, even if the church had depicted Mary as a prostitute, that would in no way have discredited her, because she was clearly depicted as a converted prostitute. The Apostle Peter himself, Brown's supposed enemy of Mary, is depicted in the New Testament as denying Jesus. Is that to discredit him? Paul too is depicted as murdering Christians in a terrible campaign of persecution. Is that to discredit him? Peter and Paul are not discredited when they are described like this, because they are forgiven sinners who have turned from their sin. As converted sinners, they actually serve as positive examples for Christians. If Mary were depicted as a prostitute in the Gospels – which she is not – then the same would apply to her as to anyone else who came to Jesus Christ for forgiveness.

## WHY DO PEOPLE WANT TO BELIEVE IT?

In short then, the central claims that Brown makes about Jesus and Mary Magdalene are incredible, and rest on no real evidence. If this is so, why do so many people want to believe the book? Why are intelligent people prepared to take it so seriously? In particular, what does the fact that people have such an enthusiasm for it as a novel and are often prepared to accept it as good history tell us about our own times? I suggest that it tells us two things.

First, it reminds us of the truth of a verse from the Book of Ecclesiastes in the Old Testament which says that God has 'set eternity in the hearts of men' (Ecclesiastes 3:11). In other words, all people are religious. This may surprise you, especially if you consider yourself to be a non-religious person, say an atheist or an agnostic. But I mean what I say. We all have gods. The strongest atheist has gods in his or her life. We are all worshippers of something. The verse from Ecclesiastes tells us that God has made us religious creatures, that he has set eternity in all of our hearts. This is why we can find no true satisfaction apart from God, and why people are attracted to the religious element that runs through books like *The Da Vinci Code*. We have an inkling that there is something more, and we are intrigued by it. We are drawn to turning the pages to find out more.

But the second thing that the popularity of *The Da Vinci Code* tells us about our age is darker and harder to hear. I am interested here not just in why people find books with religion in them attractive, but why people find Dan Brown's specific version of religion attractive. Here the answer is more unsettling. Why do people favour this kind of religiosity? Because many are looking for religion, but religion on their own terms, cheap religion. Many of us want religion, but we want religion that is comfortable, religion which will not involve us accepting hard truths about ourselves, religion which will allow us to continue running our own lives our way. And this Dan Brown offers. In fact, if you did take the religion you find in the book seriously, if you did take Dan Brown's characters as your guides, you would perhaps change something in your life: you might embrace ritualized sexual activity. The *hieros gamos* rite stands at the heart of the sacred feminine spirituality which he advocates. We are all religious, and *The Da Vinci Code* offers us cost-free sensual religion.

# Chapter 2

# Mary Magdalene: Witness?

RELIABLE HISTORY?

*T*he problem, as we have seen, is that the convenient cost-free religion of Dan Brown's novel is not true. It is based on wild and unsubstantiated historical claims. At this point I want to ask what the New Testament itself offers us in the witness of the real Mary Magdalene which it contains. Before we do that, however, we need to face up to a question. We have subjected Dan Brown's picture of Jesus to historical scrutiny. What happens when we subject the Gospels of the New Testament to the same kind of scrutiny? Can they stand up to such examination? Is there any reason to believe that their picture of Jesus Christ is true?

## CORRUPTED MANUSCRIPTS?

The first question we need to ask here concerns the ancient copies of the Gospels which have survived and on which our modern translations are based. Are these manuscripts reliable copies of the originals? Were they corrupted in transmission?

A basic answer to this question is easily given because it is possible to compare manuscripts from different periods of time and from distant places to see if a major variation has been introduced at some point. In fact there are more than 2,300 surviving manuscripts of all or part of the Gospels from the earliest Christian centuries. Comparing these Gospel manuscripts reveals only two passages where the textual evidence is sufficiently uncertain to question the wording of more than a verse or two, namely Mark 16:9ff. and John 7:53-8:11. With the other shorter variations the established principles of textual criticism normally make clear what the correct reading should be. Significant differences between the manuscripts are noted at the bottom of the page in a good edition of the Bible, so there is nothing being hidden here.

It is estimated by experts that 97-99% of the original text of the Gospels is known to us in its original wording. In the remaining verses the uncertainties do not affect any fundamental aspects of the Christian faith. We may explain this accuracy by remembering that the Christians who copied the manuscripts through the ages themselves thought that the text they were reproducing was the very words of God himself, which would be enough to make anyone work carefully.

While speaking of manuscripts, it is also revealing to note how strong the manuscript tradition is for the New Testament compared to other ancient documents. Among the New Testament manuscripts which include the Gospels, two of the more extensive ones, known as Codex Vaticanus and Codex Sinaiticus, date back to about AD350, just under 300 years from when the Gospels were first written. The John Rylands papyrus fragment, a portion of John 18, dates back to around AD125. Compare this with other ancient documents, documents on which we rely for much of our knowledge of ancient history. We have only nine or ten good manuscripts of Caesar's *Gallic Wars*. The earliest of them comes from around 900 years after Caesar wrote. We have thirty-five books of the ancient historian Livy, but they survive in not more than twenty manuscripts of any worth. Only one of them goes back as far as around 400 years after he actually wrote the text. Of the surviving portions of the *Histories* and *Annals* by Tacitus we have only two manuscripts. The earliest comes from the ninth century, about 800 years after he wrote. There is no comparison here: 2,300 manuscripts of the Gospels compared to nine, twenty, and two of the works of these authors; around 350 years until the first good manuscripts of the Gospels, compared to around 900, 400 or 800 with these authors. A table shows the figures at a glance:

| Text | Approximate interval between writing and our first manuscript | Number of copies |
|------|---------------------------------------------------------------|------------------|
| Julius Caesar *Gallic Wars* | 900 years | 9-10 |
| Livy *History of Rome* | 400 years | 20 |
| Tacitus *Histories* and *Annals* | 800 years | 2 |
| The Gospels | 300 years | >2,300 |

This data shows that by the standards of ancient history we have far more manuscript evidence for the Gospels than for any of these classic works. In fact, if anyone wishes to claim that the manuscript evidence for the Gospels is weak, he or she will have to reject huge swathes of ancient history as well.

## INCREDIBLE MIRACLES?

If the content of the Gospels was reliably copied and we have what was originally written, is what was originally written credible? The first question to ask here concerns miracles.

Large portions of all four New Testament Gospels are taken up with accounts of the miracles Jesus performed. There were more than thirty of them, excluding the miraculous things that happened to Jesus, for example his resurrection from the dead. If we have to reject miracles, we certainly have to reject the Gospels.

The most obvious reason to reject miracles is that they violate the regular 'laws of nature', laws established by everyday and scientific observation. Philosophers like David Hume have expressed this view when they have defined miracles as 'violations' of the laws of nature, a description intended to show that they cannot happen. Hume inferred from repeated observation that the laws of nature are supported by so much evidence that it would be impossible to have a sufficient amount of counter-evidence to believe in a miracle. There are at least two ways in which this scepticism is flawed.

Firstly, if we grant that the God of the Bible exists then there will be no problem in holding to the rationality of believing in miracles. This is because God in the first place created the entire universe including the laws of nature. As their creator he is quite able to alter or suspend them. Moreover, the God of the Bible is not only the creator of the universe, but also its sustainer, so that to speak of the laws of nature as being 'violated' by him gives them too much independence from him. They depend on his sustaining work for their moment-to-moment existence. This argument does not of course show that miracles happen, but it does show that within the Christian view of the world their occurrence is perfectly reasonable.

Secondly, the scientific method itself should allow at least the possibility of miracles. Scientific enquiry must always be open to the possibility of new evidence. If the scientist proceeds by observing what happens and shaping laws around such observation, then he cannot rule out certain events prior to observing them. He may think certain kinds of new event very unlikely, but he may not rule them out as impossible. Science may only say what has been observed and what will most likely be observed, it may not say what cannot be observed. This view is in fact increasingly popular with scientists themselves, largely as a result of the dramatic surprises that they keep encountering in the universe. On its own terms, therefore, science ought to allow the possibility that there is a creator God who may accelerate, alter, or suspend the laws of nature, even if it regards such events as highly improbable.

## CHINESE WHISPERS?

But even if we grant the possibility of miracles, was there not such a long gap between the events of Jesus's life and the writing of the Gospels that a serious game of Chinese whispers could have taken place? Taking the widest range of opinions, there were probably twenty to sixty years between Jesus's life and their being written. This naturally makes the modern mind suspect that there was time for serious corruption of the record to occur.

In modern cultures this would be an entirely reasonable suspicion. If no one at the time had written down anything about the Gulf War you could be sure that accounts suddenly recorded twenty to sixty years later would be highly exaggerated. But to understand the New Testament we must examine it against the background of its own culture, not ours. It would in fact be grossly anachronistic to fail to do so.

First century culture was obviously radically different from our own. It lacked all means of instant easy recording and recall and relied on oral tradition much more heavily than we do. But this also meant that oral tradition was a more reliable medium because memorization was regularly practised. Some even esteemed oral tradition *above* written records. In fact, on this count the first century was more like contemporary Islamic cultures where the Qu'ran is memorized in its entirety.

Let me be more specific. We know that the Jewish teachers or rabbis after about AD70 made their disciples memorize the teaching by which they should live, termed *halakah*. Rabbis would often use memorable forms to aid this process. Indeed, there were professional memorizers called *tannaim*. It is interesting that Jesus is often called 'Rabbi' in the Gospels, though he did not hold the office formally. Presumably therefore he was called 'Rabbi' because he acted and taught like a rabbi. If this method of rabbinic teaching existed before AD70, then the Gospels are most likely founded on the teaching of the Rabbi Jesus memorized by his disciples during his ministry.

Even if we cannot infer how Jesus would have taught from later rabbinic practice, we do know for sure that teachers in Palestine and indeed in the Graeco-Roman world as a whole followed a particular educational method. This involved gathering around themselves a group of disciples who would listen carefully to the teacher and learn from his example. The disciples would then themselves continue the same teaching and way of life. Jesus was clearly viewed as a teacher and he is frequently described as teaching in the Gospels. We may, therefore, expect that he provided for the preservation of his words in the same way as other teachers of his time. It is then no surprise that much of the teaching of Jesus is arranged in a deliberately memorable form. One example would be Mark 8:35: 'whoever would save his life will lose it; and whoever loses his life for my sake and the gospel's will save it'. Given the importance of Jesus's way of life for his disciples, the concern for preserving an accurate record would also have extended beyond his words to his deeds.

We must go further. The disciples considered Jesus to be more than just another rabbi or teacher. They believed that he was a prophet like Moses, more, that he was the

Messiah himself, the saviour of Israel. Given these convictions, they would have sought to preserve his teachings and the memory of his life with great care since they judged him to be the Word and Wisdom of God himself.

We may conclude, therefore, that the material we have in the Gospels was passed down in a culture highly suited to its reliable preservation, and that it stemmed ultimately from the memorization of eye-witnesses. To think that the memory of Jesus could have been doctored freely by the early church is to fail to grasp both the nature of the culture at the time and the commitment of the early disciples to the historical Jesus.

## Early Written Accounts

Yet even this is only half the story. While the culture of the time was largely oral, there are good reasons to think that the teachings of Jesus would soon have been written down in documents which we no longer have, but which were used by the Gospel writers. There are two key arguments here.

First, Luke himself states at the outset of his Gospel that 'Many have undertaken to draw up an account of the things that have been fulfilled among us, just as they were handed down to us by those who from the first were eyewitnesses and servants of the word' (Luke 1:1-2). The word used for 'draw up' (*anatassomai*) implies that his Gospel is based on previous written accounts.

Secondly, other groups that existed in New Testament times quickly composed their religious works in written form, for example the group at Qumran who produced the Dead Sea Scrolls. Indeed, elementary education, which was widespread in Palestine, entailed the memorization of the written Scriptures and other written texts important to the community. It is thus likely that there would have been an early move to write an account of the life and teaching of Jesus.

Contrary to the popular belief, the disciples could have been well-qualified to do this. They certainly need not have been uneducated. James and John the sons of Zebedee were from a family wealthy enough to own boats and hire servants (Mark 1:19-20), and Levi (called Matthew, and, according to early Christians, the author of the Gospel bearing his name) was a tax-collector, an unpopular but able man.

To the reliability of the oral tradition and the existence of early written sources we must add a third factor, the authority of the early Christian eye-witnesses. In the Acts of the Apostles Luke describes how the teaching of Paul was tested by the council of apostles and elders in Jerusalem (Acts 15:6-29). Here is an example of the early Christian teaching of Paul being tested by the original apostles who knew Jesus. If this was the practice of the early church then it would have been difficult for the record of Jesus's life and teachings to have been twisted or exaggerated under the scrutiny of such eye-witnesses. We may safely say that the history of Jesus was preserved in a reliable oral and written form and was tested by eyewitnesses.

## DIGGING FOR EVIDENCE

Having discussed the nature of the Gospels, it is also useful to look for archaeological findings that support their accounts of the life of Jesus. This evidence is obviously limited because you could not find archaeological evidence that Jesus spoke certain words. It is also limited by the inevitable effects of physical ruin and decay. This is particularly the case in Jerusalem, where much of the Gospel narrative takes place, because the city was destroyed by the Romans in AD70. Nonetheless, there have been some remarkable finds which have confirmed incidental details in the Gospels.

In Mark 2:1-12 we read of how Jesus healed a paralysed man in Capernaum. The man's friends lowered him through a hole in the roof of the house because there were too many people inside it for them to reach Jesus. Excavations in Capernaum have revealed houses where the roofs were made of removable mud and branches, and where an external stair-case would have allowed access even when the inside of the house was full.

John 4:5 mentions the well at Sychar (now a village called 'Askar). This well is still there. More strikingly, John uses two words for it, *pēgē* (v. 5) and *phrear* (vv. 11, 12). The first denotes a running spring or fountain, the second a dug-out well. Both parts survive.

John 5:2 describes the pool at Bethesda with five porticoes. This has been excavated. It stands in the north-east quarter of the Old City near Nehemiah's 'Sheep Gate', and has indeed five porticoes, four surrounding the pools with a fifth separating them.

More examples of such incidental details could be given, but let me summarise the picture so far. I have argued that we have in our manuscripts a reliable version of what was originally written in the Gospels. There are no rational problems with believing in miracles in the light of God's existence and the methods of modern science. The Gospels were composed on the basis of a stable oral tradition and written sources dating back to the days of Jesus himself. These would have been monitored by eyewitnesses in the early church, and some of the details in them are confirmed by archaeological discoveries.

## MARY'S WITNESS

With these arguments for the reliability of the Gospels in place, we return now to Mary, to see how she is actually a *central* character in the New Testament, not a suppressed dissenter, and to ask what she tells us about the eternity we find in our hearts.

The most important scenes where Mary Magdalene appears in the Gospels are at the death and resurrection of Jesus. She saw

Jesus die and she saw Jesus rise. This makes her very significant indeed. To grasp the importance of Mary as a witness of the death and resurrection of Jesus it is necessary to understand the importance of those events themselves. We turn therefore to examine why, according to the Bible, the death and resurrection of Jesus are the central events of history. With this in mind we will be able to grasp how significant it is that Mary was there as a witness.

Why did Jesus die? Why is Mary seeing him die so significant? As I write, *The Da Vinci Code* is being made into a film. Another recent film which provoked people to consider the identity of Jesus Christ was Mel Gibson's *The Passion of the Christ*. I am told that at the start of that film these words from Isaiah, an Old Testament prophet, were emblazoned across the screen:

> He was pierced for our transgressions, he was crushed for our iniquities; the punishment that brought us peace was upon him, and by his wounds we are healed. (Isaiah 53:5)

Much has been written in criticism of Gibson's film, but he had at least this right. These words take us to the heart of the Christian faith and the meaning of Jesus's death. But we need to start a step back to understand them. What are 'transgressions' and 'iniquities'? Jesus Christ explained such words when he taught that every human being produces evil from within, from the heart (for example in Mark 7:14-23). In some of us this evil is very evident in outward deeds – murder, theft, violence etc. You may well know people of whom you think that this is obviously true! The rest of us, however, look quite moral on the outside for much of the time. But Jesus taught that our hearts are still twisted. He taught that our greatest evil is to turn away from the God who made us, to flee, as he put it in the parable of the prodigal son, from our creator-father.

God, a holy God, does not overlook this evil. Yet in his love, he does not desire the death of his creatures. He does not desire that we should ourselves be punished with the eternal punishment we deserve for such a grave offence. So in his love he sent his Son, Jesus Christ, to suffer and die on the cross in the place of sinners. And the Son, loving his people as his Father loved them, willingly came to be pierced for their evil, to be crushed for their iniquity. He stood in their place and willingly took the punishment deserved by them. He was substituted for his people. Their punishment was transferred to him.

Perhaps you believe that already – if you do you can see why Mary seeing the crucifixion means so much. The crucifixion as the Bible explains it is *the* great central moment in human history. Here is God's only Son sent as the Saviour, accomplishing his great plan of love. Here is the moment when the sin of billions of people is lifted up and carried by Jesus Christ on his own shoulders as he is cut off from his Father and dies in their place. Jesus in his love takes all of this from his people. And standing watching is a woman, seeing the terrible outward, bloody effects of this agonizing punishment. Unlike all but one of the male disciples, Mary stayed with Jesus and became a witness to this central event of human history.

And what happens next with Mary and Jesus after his body has been taken down and removed to a tomb? She returns to his tomb on the third day, the Sunday. And there she finds not the body of Jesus but the risen Jesus himself:

> So the women hurried away from the tomb, afraid yet filled with joy, and ran to tell his disciples. Suddenly, Jesus met them. 'Greetings,' he said. They came to him, clasped his feet and worshipped him. (Matthew 28:9)

Mary then runs to the other disciples, as the first person in human history to bear witness to the resurrection of Jesus Christ from the dead. Here is a detail that no one would have invented, given that women had no legal status as witnesses:

> Mary Magdalene went to the disciples with the news: 'I have seen the Lord!' And she told them that he had said these things to her. (John 20:18).

Why did Jesus rise? Why is Mary seeing him rise so significant? Note how Mary announced his resurrection: 'I have seen the Lord!'. By raising Jesus from the dead, God made him Lord of the entire world, of the whole creation. Mary knew this: she knew that she had seen the 'Lord', a term used in the Old Testament for God himself. Mary was the first human being in history to see that Jesus Christ had by his resurrection been made the exalted Lord of the entire universe.

It makes no sense to think that Mary has been side-lined by the church when she stands as a witness to the crucifixion of Jesus which is at the centre of history. The cross of Christ is the only means God has appointed for our rescue, the only way we can find forgiveness for all the things we have done wrong, for our rejection of God. And it makes no sense to think that she has been side-lined when she stands as the very first witness to the resurrection of Jesus, the event by which he has been made Lord of all.

So what does the real Mary of history say to you today? Not that she was married to Jesus and had children whose descendants walk the streets of modern France. No, she speaks to us as a witness. She tells us that the cross of Jesus is the place where we can find complete cleansing and forgiveness. She tells us that he has been made Lord of all. She invites you to come with her to the cross, to leave your sins there, to bow with her before

Jesus Christ, to worship him as your Lord just as she did. Here is the true Mary described in the authentic documents, and here is the true Jesus to whom she points, the only Saviour and the only Lord.

# Further Reading and Sources

If it is the vital question of the identity of Jesus Christ which has sparked your interest, then I would encourage you to go back to the primary texts themselves. As we have seen, the texts which stand closest to Jesus and bear faithful witness to him are not the later Gnostic Gospels, written long after his life, death and resurrection. They are rather the four New Testament Gospels themselves, Matthew, Mark, Luke, and

John, written much nearer his time either by those who knew Jesus or by those who used material from such witnesses. If you are indeed interested in the truth about Jesus Christ, why not make one of them the next book you read?

Normally academic writers are taken to be claiming originality unless they put in their text an explicit reference to someone else's work. For this piece I eschew all such automatic claims to originality. To avoid cluttering the text and to make it more accessible, I have not given any references except where I have actually quoted someone, but I do not claim that anything here other than the arrangement of the material is original. Given that I have studied theology and teach Church History for a living, much of the argument does come immediately from my own recall and reasoning rather than from other writers. But if you read further on these issues you will quickly find, as I did, that many of the points made here about *The Da Vinci Code* are reproduced in numerous books and websites. This in itself is interesting, because it shows how obvious some of the replies to Dan Brown's picture of history are. For instance, anyone who knows anything about Gnosticism would think of the replies to Claims 3 and 4 by himself within a split-second of reading the relevant part of the novel. For the more specific details of some of the argument concerning the novel itself I would like to acknowledge my particular indebtedness to two books, *Breaking the Da Vinci Code* by Darrell L. Bock (Nelson Books, 2004), and *The Da Vinci Hoax* by Carl E. Olson and Sandra Miesel (Ignatius Press, 2004). I am grateful to Ignatius Press for permission to quote from *The Da Vinci Hoax*.

The same applies to the material on the reliability of the Gospels. I have made use of details from four books in particular, which I would recommend: F.F. Bruce's *The New Testament Documents: Are They Reliable?* (Inter-Varsity Press, 2000), R.T. France's *The Evidence for Jesus* (Inter-Varsity Press, 1986), Craig Blomberg's *The Historical Reliability of the Gospels* (Inter-Varsity Press, 1987), and Paul Barnett's *Is the New Testament History?* (Paternoster Press, 1986).

Of course I do not necessarily agree with every detail in any of these books, nor do I mean to assert that their authors would agree with what I have written here.

Should you want to follow up the passages I have quoted which come from outside these texts, the one from Irenaeus may be found in *Ante-Nicene Fathers* (Hendrickson, 1995), the one from Ignatius of Antioch in *Early Christian Writings*, ed. A. Louth (Penguin Books, 1987). These two are both available online at www.ccel.org. The Gospel of Philip is in *The Nag Hammadi Library*, ed. James M. Robinson (HarperSanFrancisco, 1990).

Despite their usefulness, all of these books, like the one in your hand, will come and go. How much better, I would again suggest, to read the Book that has endured for two millennia, and that will abide for ever. I wish you happy reading!

# Christian Focus Publications
publishes books for all ages

Our mission statement –

## *STAYING FAITHFUL*
In dependence upon God we seek to help make His infallible Word, the Bible, relevant. Our aim is to ensure that the Lord Jesus Christ is presented as the only hope to obtain forgiveness of sin, live a useful life and look forward to heaven with Him.

## *REACHING OUT*
Christ's last command requires us to reach out to our world with His gospel. We seek to help fulfill that by publishing books that point people towards Jesus and help them develop a Christ-like maturity. We aim to equip all levels of readers for life, work, ministry and mission.

Books in our adult range are published in three imprints.

*Christian Focus* contains popular works including biographies, commentaries, basic doctrine and Christian living. Our children's books are also published in this imprint.

*Mentor* focuses on books written at a level suitable for Bible College and seminary students, pastors, and other serious readers. The imprint includes commentaries, doctrinal studies, examination of current issues and church history.

*Christian Heritage* contains classic writings from the past.

Christian Focus Publications, Ltd
Geanies House, Fearn, Ross-shire,
IV20 1TW, Scotland, United Kingdom
info@christianfocus.com